Letters to Barbara

Leo Meter

Letters to Barbara

with an Afterword by Barbara Meter

translated by James Agee

THE OVERLOOK PRESS

WOODSTOCK • NEW YORK

In the East, April 4th, 1943.

My dear little Barbara,

Your Papa Leo is so far away that he can't even visit you on your birthday. To be with you on the 6th, I would have to sit in a big, strong train for many, many days. I'm in a town that is much smaller than Amsterdam, and there is not as much water here either, just a little stream far down in the valley. Way up on the mountain stands a pink and white church, There are ruined houses all around. People can't live in them any more. On top of another mountain stands another church and a great big castle. The castle was destroyed too, but not recently, like the houses. It was destroyed many hundreds of years ago. I don't know who lived in it, maybe a great and rich king who ruled over many poor people. The king has been gone for a long time, but the poor people are still here, and they're still poor. They have long beards that look like fur, and long fur coats that hang down like beards. The women have cloths on their heads and very colorful skirts with dark trim.

Im Osten, 7. April 1943

Meine liebe kleine Barbara,

dein Papa Leo ist soweit weg, dass er dich nicht
einmal zu deinem Geburtstag besuchen kann.
Ganz viele Tage müsste ich in einer großen
und starken Eisenbahn sitzen, wollte ich am
6. bei Dir sein.
Ich bin hier in [Zeichnung: Eisenbahn]
einer Stadt die viel kleiner ist als Amsterdam
und soviel Wasser gibt's hier auch nicht. Nur
ein kleiner Bach tief unten im Tal und oben
auf den Berg eine   weiß und
rosa   Kirche.

Rund herum stehen Häuser die
ganz kaputt sind. Menschen
können darin nicht mehr wohnen.
Auf einem anderen Berg ist noch eine Kirche
und eine große Burg. Diese Burg ist auch kaput-
gemacht worden; aber nicht jetzt, wie die Häuser
sondern schon vor vielen hundert Jahren. Ich
weiß nicht wer da
einmal gewohnt hat,
vielleicht ein großer
und reicher König
dem viele arme
Leute gehörten. Der
König ist schon lange
weg aber die vielen Leute sind noch immer da und
auch noch immer so arm. Sie haben oft lange
Bärte die   wie Pelz aussehen und lange
Pelzmäntel die an ihnen herunter hängen wie
Bärte. Die   Frauen haben Tücher auf den Kopf und
ganz bunte Röcke mit dunklem
Rand.

Alle fahren mit kleinen Wagen und die werden gezogen von kleinen mageren Pferden. Manchmal ist ein Pferd davor aber oft auch zwei oder gar drei. Einen Panje wagen nennt man solch ein Fuhrwerk und die schwachen Pferdchen ziehen die Wagen mit ganzen Familien beladen durch den knietiefen Matsch der hier ist, wenn es nur ein klein wenig geregnet hat. Ich hätte

Dir gerne einen großen Kirschen mit Lichtchen und Spielsachen geschickt aber hier kann man nichts kaufen. Nur Eier und die kann man nicht schicken. Selbst Blümchen kann man nicht bekommen, denn hier ist es noch kalt und alle Blümchen sind noch tief in der warmen Erde versteckt. Darum muß ich Dir ein paar Blümchen auf den Brief malen, dieselben die du jedes Jahr zum Geburtstag von mir bekommen hast.

Liebe kleine Barbara, vergiß nicht deinen Papa wenn er jetzt solange nicht zu Dir kommen kann und wenn ich im Sommer nach Amsterdam komme dann geh ich mit dir spazieren und wir kaufen was schönes zum Geburtstag.

Meine Adresse ist:
Grenadier Soldat
Leo Meyer
Feldpostnummer
43143 E
Päckchen bis
hundert gramm
können frei verschickt
werden und Zigaretten
habe ich dringend
nötig.

Liebe Barbara
schreib mir bitte
mal ich schreib
dann sofort
zurück. Bis
dahin mit
vielen tausend
Geburtstags-
grüßen und küssen
Dein Papa Leo.

All the people drive around in little carriages which are drawn by small, skinny horses. Sometimes there's just one horse pulling, sometimes there are two or even three. This kind of carriage is called a *Panyeh* car, and the weak little horses drag them along through knee-deep mud, sometimes with whole families sitting on top. It takes just a little bit of rain to make the roads muddy like that. I wish I could send you a big cake with candles, and toys, but there's nothing to buy here. Just eggs, and I can't send those. I can't even get flowers, because it's still cold here, and all the flowers are still hidden deep beneath the earth. So I'll have to paint some flowers on this letter, the same kind you've always gotten from me on your birthday.

Dear little Barbara, don't forget your Papa now that he can't be with you for such a long time. When I come to visit you in Amsterdam in the summer, I will take a walk with you, and we'll buy something pretty for your birthday.

Dear Barbara, please write to me, I'll answer you right away, Till then, many thousands of birthday greetings and kisses.

Your Papaleo

My address is: Soldier Leo Meter, Field Post Number 43143E. Packages weighing up to one hundred grams may be sent free of charge, and I urgently need cigarettes.

In the East, Easter 1943.

Dear little Barbara,

Today is Easter, and everything on the fields and the streets is new, small, and young. The little flowers, the sheep, and the children. Two weeks ago, the children looked like this (. . .), and now they look like this (. . .).

A few days ago I drove far, far away in a big car to a great big forest on top of a mountain. Next to that mountain was another mountain with a forest on top, and another and another, and in the valleys between the mountains were houses and fields. The houses had straw roofs with storks on them, and chickens, pigs, and horses were in the courtyards. The people who lived there had all gone deep into the woods. I only saw one old man. He was walking all alone on a long, long street.

Im Osten, Ostern 1943

Liebe kleine Barbara,
heute ist Ostern und auf allen Feldern und Straßen
ist alles neu, klein und jung. die Blümchen,
die Schäfchen und die Kinder. Vor zwei Wochen sahen die
Kinder so aus:

und jetzt sehen sie schon so aus.

Vor wenigen
Tagen war ich
mit einem großen
Auto ganz weit weggefahren in
einen großen Wald der auf einem
Berg war. Daneben war wieder
ein Berg mit einem Wald darauf
und so weiter und dazwischen
in den Tälern waren Häuser und Felder.

die Häuser haben auf dem Dach Stroh und einen
Hof. Im Hof Hühner, Schweine und Pferdchen.
die Leute die
dort wohnen
waren alle
weit in den
Wald gegangen.
Nur einen
alten Mann

habe ich noch gesehen und der
ging ganz allein auf einer
langen langen Straße spazieren.

auf den Straßen, die sehr
breit und ganz staubig sind
gehen sonntags die Bauern
in ihren bunten Kleidern
in die Kirche. Heute am Ostertag ist es sehr
besonders festlich. Aber ich kann es nicht
sehen, denn ich muß heute den ganzen Tag zu
Hause sitzen und warten ob ich nicht wieder
ganz schnell mit dem Auto irgendwohin muß.
Trotzdem habe ich Zeit diesen Brief an Dich zu schreiben.
An anderen Tagen muß ich sehr viel arbeiten
und habe ganz wenig Zeit zu schreiben, aber
denken tue ich viel an meine kleine Barbara
und oft bin ich bang, daß Du mich beinahe
vergessen hast oder nicht mehr kennst wenn
ich im Sommer für ein paar Tage nach
Amsterdam komme. Einen ganz kleinen Papa Leo
habe ich dir hierhin gezeichnet in einem neuen
Anzug mit einem Hut und großen schwarzen Schuhen.
Das habe ich getan damit Du nicht bang
bist vor mir wenn ich komme, denn
dann werde ich den neuen Anzug anhaben
und dann werden wir zusammen
spazieren gehen und für Dich viele
schöne Sachen kaufen.

Liebe Barbara,
bald schreibe ich Dir wieder einen
Brief. Viele viele Osterküsse
von Deinem Papa Leo.

On the streets, which are very wide and dusty, the peasants go to church on Sundays in their colorful clothes. I'm sure this Easter day is especially festive. But I can't go out to watch, for I have to stay home all day and wait in case I have to go somewhere very quickly by car. That's why I have time to write this letter to you. On other days I have to work a lot and don't have much time to write; but I think a lot about my little Barbara, and I often worry that you may have nearly forgotten me or will no longer know me when I come to Amsterdam for a few days. I've made a picture for you of a very small Papaleo in his new suit with an iron hat and big black shoes. I did this so that you won't be frightened when I come, because then I'll be wearing this new suit. When I come, we will go for a walk together, and I'll buy you many beautiful things.

Dear Barbara, I will write you another letter soon. Many, many Easter kisses from

Your Papaleo

In the East, July 4th, 1943, the first beautiful Sunday in many days

Dear little Barbara, next to my bed lies a little picture, a photograph of you, and early in the morning I sometimes look at it and say "Hello" to you. But then I have to quickly wash, brush my teeth, and get dressed. It's not like at home here, there aren't any faucets with hot and cold water, there's only a deep well, and I have to draw up all the water I need with a pail. The pail stands in front of the house in the courtyard. When I want to take a bath, I can't get into a lovely white glistening tub like you, I have to first walk to the bathhouse—it's called a sauna here. The sauna is a house, and inside is a room full of hot steam. When I have undressed, I go into the room, and there I pour hot and then cold water over my head from a wooden bucket, sputtering and shaking myself and breaking into a tremendous sweat. Then I go home, feeling very tired but also very clean.

I can't tell you much about breakfast, only that our coffee pot is huge. It has to hold enough coffee for ten soldiers who are always very thirsty. In the morning I always eat up all my food, because in the afternoon we get new bread and new butter.

After eating, I go to work, and sometimes work is hard for me, not because the work is hard,

Liebe kleine Barbara,

Neben meinem Blatt liegt ein kleines Bildchen, ein Foto von Dir, und morgens früh seh ich es mir immer einmal an und sag dir "Guten Tag". Aber dann muß ich mich ganz schnell fertig machen. Waschen, die Zähne putzen und anziehen. Hier ist es nicht eine Zuhause, hier läuft kein kaltes und heißes Wasser aus dem Wasserhahn, nein, hier gibt es nur einen tiefen Ziehbrunnen und kaltes Wasser muß ich erst herziehen in meinem Eimer. Der Brunnen steht vor dem Haus im Hof. Wenn ich baden will, kann ich auch nicht einfach in so eine schöne weiße blitzblanke Badewanne steigen wie Du, ich muß zuerst einen Spaziergang zur Badeanstalt machen, darum fehlt die Zeit. Die Badanne ist im Haus und darin ist ein Zimmer, das ist ganz voll mit heißem Dampf. Wenn ich mich ausgezogen habe, gehe ich in das Zimmer und da schütte ich mir aus Holzeimern die die Frauen heißes und dann kaltes Wasser über den Kopf, prusste und schüttle mich und schwitze ganz schrecklich. Wenn ich dann nach Hause gehe bin ich ganz munter und auch sauber.

Vom Kriegsstück kann ich dir nicht viel erzählen, nur das deutere Wasserkannen riesengroß ist. Für gehe Soldaten, die künst haben muß man reichen. Morgens esse ich immer alles auf was ich noch habe, denn am Nachmittag gibt es schon wieder nötig zwei und meine Mutter.

Nach dem Essen gehe ich arbeiten und die Arbeit fällt mir manchesmal schwer, nicht weil die Arbeit schwer ist

sondern weil ich nicht immer mit meinen Gedanken
dabei bin; die sind dann bei dir liebe Babuschka.
Ich denke dann an all die Geschichten die wir immer
zusammen gesungen haben; aber wenn ich noch heute
kommen kann ich dir so viele schöne Geschichten erzählen
von den kleinen Bübchen und Mädchen die hier
wohnen. Von den bunten Kleidern habe ich dir
schon erzählt aber noch nichts von den schönen roten
haarschleifen der kleinen Mädchen. An zwei langen
Zöpfen ums Gesicht so gezogen sie durch die
Steppe, auf dem Rücken tragen sie ihr Einkauf-
körbchen.

Oft haben sie auch
einen Krug in der
Hand in der sie die
Suppe oder die Milch
mitnehmen.
Für die Suppe
haben sie keinen
Schrank sondern

sie werden auf den Zaun gesteckt, der
trocknen sie von selbst und sie werden
sie aufbewahrt. Für das essen haben
sie Leute einen ganz komischen Schrank.
Er ist ein Loch in die Erde hinein-
gebaut steht draußen vor dem Haus
und ist von außen grün mit Gras bewachsen.

das essen, die Milch die Butter
und der Käse bleibt
darinnen schön kühl und frisch.
Es ist beinahe wie ein Eisschrank.
Bis jetzt hätte man auch noch keinen
Eisschrank nötig gehabt denn die letzte Zeit so sehr
sind geregnet. aber heute ist es wieder schöner

Sonntag
mit Sonne
und mit
Wind.
Vor ein
paar Tagen
bin ich mit
der Eisenbahn
zu andern

Verwandten gefahren die in einem Holzhäuschen mitten in

but because in my thoughts I am far away, with you, my dear little Babushka. Then I think of all the stories we always sang together; but when I come home, I will tell you many beautiful stories about the little boys and girls who live here. I already told you about the colorful clothes, but I haven't told you about the pretty bows the little girls wear in their hair. Two long braids tied with one bow, that's how they walk through the town, with their shopping baskets on their backs. Often they're holding a jug full of soup or milk. They don't put the jugs in a cupboard, they stick them on a fence post to dry, and that's where they're kept. The people put their food in a very funny kind of cupboard. It's outside in front of the house, built into the earth and completely overgrown with grass. It's almost like a refrigerator—the food, the milk, the butter, and the eggs, everything stays fresh and cool in there.

Until today, people wouldn't have needed a refrigerator, for it has been raining all through the week, but now the weather is nice again, plenty of sun and lots of wind. A few days ago I took a train to visit some other soldiers living in a wooden house in the middle of

the woods.
There I picked strawberries, which grow wild by the edge
of the forest. There is a big bird living with the soldiers. His
name is Jacob. Jacob is very wild, and he bites and
scratches when you try to stroke him. If you give him milk
soup with blueberries, he doesn't want it; young green
peas with scrambled eggs, he won't even touch; he
wouldn't even eat vanilla ice cream with strawberries and
whipped cream. What he's really licking his beak for are
those lovely bright little songbirds. That's why the soldiers
want to send Jacob away soon. Then he won't be allowed to stay in the pretty wooden house and hear the
beautiful songs the cossack soldiers sing in the evening.

Wald wohne.
dort bin ich
hübschen
geglückt
die dort
wild am
Waldrande
wachsen.
Die drei Soldaten
wohnt auch ein großer Vogel der heißt Jakob.
Jakob ist sehr wild und beißt und kratzt wenn
man ihn streicheln
will. Die leckersten
Milchsuppe mit
Blaubeeren
will er nicht,
junge grüne
Erbsen mit
Zucker rührt er
nicht an sogar

Vanilla eis mit Erdbeeren und Schlagsahne
würde er nicht essen. nur nach den kleinen
lieben bunten Singvögeln lüstet er sich den
Schnabel. darum wollen die Soldaten Jakob auch
bald

verschicken. Er darf dann nicht mehr im schönen
Holzhaus bleiben wo die Kosakken Soldaten
abends so schöne Lieder singen.

Lieber Dabbalor, ich habe mich sehr gefreut als flisderbag geschrieben hat, daß Du mich noch nicht vergessen hast. Vielleicht dauert es jetzt gar nicht mehr so sehr lange und wir gehen zusammen spazieren. Wenn die Reise zu dir nicht so lange dauern würde, würde ich dir ja ganz viele Tiere und Blumen mitbringen. Hier gibt es so viele Frösche, Kröten, Eichhörnchen und lange Schlangen.

Aber ich werde nicht mit leeren Händen kommen. Wir müssen dann zusammen in Amsterdam versuchen ob wir noch schönes für dich finden. Bis dahin viele liebe Grüße von

Deinem Leopapi

Liebste Elisabeth, inzwischen wirst du wohl Post von mir bekommen haben. Ich habe dir davon auch mit-geteilt wie ich das Geld dazu unternommen habe. Deinen Brief habe ich gestern bekommen. Herzlichen Dank! Wenn alles gut geht komme ich im August meinen Urlaub abwarten. Wie lange ich dann bleiben kann weiß ich nicht. Hoffentlich Marthe. Ich bitte daß ich ihr schon ungezählte Briefe geschrieben habe. Sie müssen habe ich zurückbekommen weil ich die Adresse

Dear Babbela, I was very happy to read in Elizabeth's letter that you haven't forgotten me yet. Maybe it won't be long now and we can walk together. If it didn't take so long to travel to where you are, I would bring you lots of animals and flowers. There are so many here. Frogs, toads, squirrels, and long snakes. But I will have to come with empty hands. So we'll have to try and find something nice for you in Amsterdam. Until then, many loving kisses from

Your Papaleo

Dear Elizabeth, by now I imagine you will have gotten my letter. In it, I told you what I've done about the money. I got your letter today. Thank you! If everything goes well, I can expect to go on furlough in August. I don't know how long I'll be able to stay. Please tell Martha that I've already written her countless letters. Most of them were returned to me because I had written the wrong address. With many good wishes and greetings,

Your Leo

In the evening, July 9, 1943.

My dear little one,

Today, for a change, I won't tell you how things look here. Instead I'll tell you about Cologne, where you have never been. Do you remember how often we talked about visiting your grandmother in Cologne *na de oorlog* (after the war)? We'll definitely do that, but Cologne won't look the way it used to, because it has been destroyed by the war, and that's why I want to tell you about what it used to be like there.

There once were some men with beards and women with long blonde hair who selected the most beautiful spot on the great river Rhine and lived there for a long time. Then many soldiers came from the south. First they fought against the bearded men, but then they got along. They built themselves a castle, a big wall around all the houses, and a temple. They fired beautiful pots, made wine and grew vegetables, married one another, and had children. The soldiers from the south brought with them an empress and many pious men. But after many years there was a quarrel between the people from the south and the people of the north, an in the end, all the soldiers had to leave in a great hurry. When they were all gone and the empress was dead, the pious men who had stayed behind made up with the bearded men, and together they all continued building the city. They built for many hundreds of years. They built beautiful houses, castles, great churches, palaces, the dome, and around all these things, to prevent anyone from hurting the city or the people who lived there, they built a great wall with magnificent gates and called the city

Lieber Klein,

heute will ich dir mal nicht erzählen wie es eine aufsicht war ich bin, sondern wie Köln war du ja noch nie warst. Weißt du noch wie oft wir davon gesprochen haben daß wir uns de oorlog zusammen nach Köln zur Großmutter fahren wollten. Das werden wir auch nur noch Köln nicht mehr so aussehen wie früher weil ab jetzt im Krieg ganz kaputt gegangen ist und darum will ich dir erzählen wie es früher dort war.

Es waren einmal Männer mit Bärten und Frauen mit langen blonden Haaren die haben sich am großen Rhein den schönsten Platz gesucht und wohnten dort lange Zeit. Dann kamen aus dem Süden viele Soldaten. Zuerst kämpften sie mit den Bart-männern, dann aber vertrugen sie sich. Sie bauten eine Burg eine große Mauer um alle Häuser herum und wurden Freunde. Sie haben schöne Töpfe getöpfert dann und Gemüse gebaut untereinander gehandelt und Kinder bekommen. Mit den Soldaten waren aus dem Süden eine Kaiserin und viele fromme Männer gekommen. Aber nach vielen Jahren gab es Streit zwischen denen aus dem Süden und dann von Norden und das Ende war das alle

Soldaten eilends wieder weg mußten. Als alle weg waren und die Kaiserin tot und die frommen Männer aber die zurückgeblieben waren wieder gut Freund mit den Bartgängern bauten alle zusammen weiter an der Stadt. Sie bauten viele hundert Jahre. Sie bauten schöne Häuser, bauten große Kirchen zuletzt den Dom und um das alles herum damit immer wieder etwas der Stadt und der Menschen die dort wohnen zuleide tun kann eine große Mauer mit gewaltigen Toren und nannten die Stadt

Colonia Claudia Agrippa   Agrip[...]

St. Martin

Rhenus fluvius

die Männer wurden immer reicher, ihre Kinder [...]
[...] die Stadt immer schöner und größer und [...]
[...] sich die Männer [...] und damit führen sie [...]
[...] und die halben München [...]

und Kaffee mit herrlichem Essen
und Gewürze. Viele hundert
Jahre haben die Bewohner der
Hansestadt Köln das Geld ihrer
Wörter [...] oder aus[...]
gegeben aber immer wenn sie
gutgelaunt hatten ihren Schatz
am Essen und trinken und bei
lustigen Geschichten. Weil die Leute Geld genug
zum Leben hatten, hatten sie auch Zeit zu Spaß [...]

vor allen Dingen die Geburtstag [...]
einen schönen Blumenstrauß [...]
und dann seinen Blumen [...]
er gebrauchte sie zum folgenden [...]

Colonia Claudia Agrippa Agrippinensis.
The men became more and more rich, their children became soldiers, priests, and eventually merchants, the city
became bigger and bigger and more and more beautiful,
and a hundred churches stretched their high towers over
the thick city walls to the sky.

The men built great ships, and on these ships they went
to where the black, the brown, and the yellow people
live, and from there they brought back strange and precious stones and cloths and marvelous food and spices.
For many hundreds of years, the people of Cologne in-
creased their fathers' wealth or else gobbled it up, but
always they were of good spirits and enjoyed

eating and drinking and telling funny stories. Because the people had enough money to live on, they also had time for fun and games. For example, there was the painter (. . .) who looked up those who had a birthday, a wedding, or some other party and brought them a beautiful bunch of flowers, ate and drank his fill, and then took the flowers away again when he left. Then he would use them for the next party.

This is Father Rhine holding the coat of arms of the city of Cologne. On the top of the shield are three crowns, because the Three Holy Kings are buried in Cologne, and below the crowns are eleven flames, because eleven thousand pious virgins are buried there.

dann ist da noch der Hummes der Tünnes und der
Schtemm. Der Schtemm ging einmal über die Straße
und da sieht er die den Hümmes ankommen und
zehn Schritte dahinter den Tünnes. Beide tief ge-
bückt, schwitzend und stöhnend. Der Schtemm reibt sich
die Augen aus dem Kopf, er zweifelt sein Zeug,
er kann sich nicht erklären was mit den beiden
los ist; denn sieht ist es doch gar nicht. Er muss
sie fragen was mit ihnen ist. Kaum aber hat er
sein Frage getan, so schauen Hummes und Tünnes
ihn an als ob er krank wäre und antworten,
ausgert: "Wir tragen doch den Deutkam weg!"
Und als Schtemm sagt er könne keinen Balken
sehen, stehen die beiden ganz dumm da und
dümmer sagt: "Oh je, jetzt haben wir den
Balken vergessen!" Da so sind die Kölner.

Wenn wir aber zusammen in Köln sind werde
ich dir eine ganze Menge Geschichten erzählen
können. Dann kann ich dir zeigen wo ich gewesen
habe als ich noch ganz klein war wo ich zur
Schule gegangen bin und alle Plätze wo ich
gerne war. Liebe Babüsch, jetzt ist der Tag
und auch das Papier zu Ende. Alles geht schlafen
die Vögel und auch das Licht und dein Jagelos
auch. Die schön braun mein liebes Kindchen
schlaf schön. Viele viele Küsschen von
deinem Bagalos.

Then there is the story of Hannes, Tunnes, and Besteva. One day Besteva was crossing the street when he saw Hannes coming along, and ten feet behind him was Tunnes, both of them bent over, sweating and groaning. Besteva stared till his eyes almost popped from his head. He raked his brain and couldn't figure out what those two might be doing. But no sooner did he ask them then Hannes and Tunnes looked at him as if he was sick in the head: "We're carrying the beam!" they said. And when Besteva said he couldn't see the beam, the other two stood there looking very foolish, until Tunnes said: "Oh dear, we forgot the beam!" Yes, that's what the people of Cologne are like.

But when we're in Cologne together, I'll be able to tell you a whole lot of stories. Then I can show you where I lived when I was a little boy, where I went to school, and all the little places where I liked to be. Dear Babusch, now the day and this sheet of paper are both at an end. Everyone is going to sleep, the birds and the light, and your Papaleo too. Be a good little girl, my dear child, sleep well. Many, many kisses from

Your Papaleo

This noon, July 17, 1943, is the first time in several days that it hasn't rained here. I have a big fat stomach from eating bean soup.

Dear little Barbara,

After eating so much thick soup, I always dream all sorts of silly things. This noon for example I dreamed that my dear little Barbara had been a bad girl. That she had broken all the pretty little animals. You and I were in a big beautiful house, and in the house were many animals. A fox and a rabbit, a frog and goldfish, a goose and a sparrow, a rooster and a little mouse. Since your Papaleo had to work, you were allowed to play with the animals all by yourself. "But," I said, "don't break anything, otherwise I'll have to scold you."

But Barbara wasn't nice at all, she broke all the animals in half, and because your Papa was just coming home, you tried to fix them again, but being in a hurry, you did it all wrong. When I first entered the room, I just had to laugh, for there in the bathtub was the little mouse with a goldfish tail, and on the edge stood the goldfish with the mouse's tail, screaming and crying.

Heute mittag am 17. Juli ...
habe ich seit vielen Tagen zum ...
... ich
habe immer ganz dicken ...
... der ...

Liebes Barbara Kindchen.
Wenn ich so viel dicke Suppe
gegessen habe, träume ich ganz
dumme Sachen. Da habe ich
heute Mittag geträumt mein liebes kleines Barbara
wär bös gewesen. All die lieben Tierchen hätte sie
kaputt gemacht. Wir waren, sie und ich in
einem großen schönen Haus. In dem Haus waren
viele Tiere. Ein Fisch und ein Kaninchen
ein Hecht und ein Goldfisch, eine Ente ein
... ein Hahn und ein kleines ...
Mäuschen. ...

und auf dem Rand ... der Goldfisch mit dem
Mäuschen ...

Ein Goldfisch kann nur im Wasser leben, auf dem
Land und in der Luft... Dann dachte ging

es sehr gut. Er konnte
sich legen und
lecken und pflücken
... dann dachte...
Hier ist der Fuchs
sehr arm!
Doch die Gans
war nicht so
glücklich, sie
mußte immer
sie flog immer... ...
tragen.

die Henne wollte
kein frisches Gemüse
essen und das
arme Kaninchen
mußte immer
auf dem Mist-
haufen sitzen.

Ganz glücklich aber war der Frosch. Er war
verliebt in sein Hinterteil das so schön singen
und so hoch fliegen konnte. — Dann aber hat dein
... doch gefangen
... und ... fühlen
zusammen mit
... Mäuse
... kein
... richtig
ganz gemacht.

A goldfish can only laugh in the water, on land it has to cry, because it can't live there. The fox was very pleased. He could lay eggs, and no sooner were they laid than he licked and slurped and swallowed them down. Foxes really love to eat eggs! But the goose was not so happy, because wherever she flew, she had to drag a heavy fox tail behind her. The rooster did not want to eat fresh vegetables, and the poor rabbit kept having to sit on a dung-heap. But the frog was truly happy. He was in love with his own backside, which now could fly and sing so beautifully. But then your Papa scolded you after all, and with a lot of effort and care, together we put the animals back together as they were supposed to be.

The goose and the goldfish, the fox and the rabbit, the rooster and the little mouse, and finally, the sparrow and the frog. And then I woke up. The sun is still shining, and I'm glad all of that was a dream. My little Barbara is a big girl now. I'm sure she doesn't break things any more and is as kind to animals as the little children I have met here.

I'd like to tell you a quick story about that. Very early in the morning, when the sun has just risen, I can already hear him coming from afar, the little boy. Clip, clop, he goes, clip, clop, for he's riding on a big horse. The horse likes to carry the boy, and the boy is very gentle and kind to the horse. When he sees me, he laughs and says: *"Djen dobre, Pan."* Then the little girl comes with the great big oxen, and they follow

die Gans und der Goldfisch, der Fuchs und das Kaninchen

der Hase und
das Mäuschen

und ganz zuletzt auch noch der Spatz und der Frosch.
dann bin ich auch aufgewacht. Noch immer spukt
die Barma und ich bin ganz froh daß ich das
Alles geträumt habe. Die kleine Barbara ist
jetzt groß. Die macht sicher nichts mehr kaputt
und ist so lieb zu ihnen wie die kleinen
Kinder die ich hier kenne. Vorher will ich die
noch schnell erzählen. Morgens ganz früh wenn
die Sonne gerade aufgegangen ist höre ich ihn
schon von weitem ankommen, den kleinen
Jungen. Klop klop klop macht's, denn er reitet
auf einem großen Pferd, das Pferd trägt den
Kleinen gern. Er ist sehr lieb und gut zum Pferd.

wenn er mich sieht, lacht er und sagt: „Den lobe,"
Pau". Dann kommt noch das kleine Wägelchen
mit den großen Ochsen. Ganz langsam gehen

hin mit dem kleinen Mädchen. Die Ochsen
sind sehr stark. Auf dem Wagen sind
große Baumstämme aufgeladen. Das kleine
Mädchen bringt mit den großen Ochsen die
Bäume zu uns. Wenn sie kommt sagt sie:
„Hier sehre, Herr."

Das sagen hier alle Leute. Es heißt, Guten Tag,
Herr. Liebe Dorobowa, es ist zwei Uhr. Die
Mittagspause ist um und ich muß jetzt
arbeiten gehen. Arbeitest du auch ein wenig?
Vielleicht hilfst du fleißbeß deiner Mutter beim
waschen. Das kannst du doch so schön. Oder
gehst du jetzt zur Schule und klebst einen
Ball und eine Blume und bunte
Ringinchen. Wenn du einmal viel mehr
Zeit hast und du hast in der Schule schon
etwas mehr gelernt dann machst du deinen
Papa einmal einen schönen Brief.
          Liebe Herbütsch,
          Auf Wiedersehen!
     viele Küßchen
          von deinem
               Papulew.

the little girl's lead. The oxen are very strong. They are pulling a cart that is laden with big tree trunks. With the help of those oxen, the little girl brings the trees to our house. When she comes, she says: "*Djen dobre, Pan.*" Everyone says that here. It means: Good day, sir.

Dear Barbara, it's two o'clock. My lunch break is over, I have to go back to work. Do you work a little too? Maybe you help Elizabeth with dusting. You're so good at that. Or are you going to school now and pasting colored pieces of paper into the shapes of a ball and a flower? If you ever have time, lots of time, after you have learned a little more in school, you'll paint a beautiful letter for your Papa.

Dear Babusch, good bye!
Many kisses from your

Papaleo

I have moved, and on this Sunday, the 25th of July, 1943, I am writing in my new house.

Dear little one,

I want to write to you again, but I don't really know what to tell you. New things don't happen every day. But I'm writing because it makes me happy to think that after many days, you will hold this letter in your hand and look at the pictures I'm going to draw in it. Can you imagine all the things this letter will experience before it reaches you? When I finish the letter and it's crammed full of new drawings, I'll drop it into the letter box. I don't have to go far to find it. The box hangs from a wall in our living-, dining-, music-, and bedroom. In the evening a soldier takes the letter along with the other letters in the box and carries it to a little house where all the soldiers' letters from our little town are collected. There they are all put together in a big sack. One letter to Cologne, another to Berlin. Many, many letters which the soldiers have written to their families back home, and one of them is this letter to you, dear Barbara.

Ich bin umgezogen und schreibe
jetzt am Sonntag den 25. Juli 1943
in meinem Haus.

Liebes Kleines,

ich will dir wieder mal schreiben aber ich weiß eigentlich
nicht was ich dir sagen soll. Nicht jeden Tag geschieht etwas
Neues. Ich schreibe doch, weil ich mich freue daß du nach
einem Tage den Brief in der Hand halten wirst und
die Bildchen die ich herein zeichnen will anschauen wirst.
Weißt du auch, was dieser Brief voraussichtlich alles
erlebt haben wird, ehe er bei dir ist. Wenn ich den Brief
fertig habe und ganz vollgekritzelt mit vielen Zeichnungen
werfe ich ihn in den Briefkasten. Da brauche ich nicht lange
zu suchen und zu fragen. Der Kasten steht in unserem

Wohn- Speise- Musik- und Schlafzimmer.   Am Abend kommt
                                            ein Soldat der Brief
                                            mit den anderen
                                            Briefen die auch im
                                            Kasten liegen und
                                            trägt sie zu einem
                                            kleinen Gebäude
                                            alle Soldatenbriefe
                                            aus unserer kleinen
                                            Stadt gesammelt
                                            werden.

Dort kommen sie alle in einen
großen Sack. Da liegen sie
                      alle zusammen.
                      Ein Brief nach
                      Köln einer
                      nach Berlin.
                      Viele viele Briefe die die Soldaten
                      nach Hause geschrieben haben, ja und
                      darunter auch der Brief an dich
                      einen darunter.

der Park wird dann zum Bahnhof getragen, und es wird

gewartet bis der Zug kommt. Eine Stunde, zwei Stunden
einen ganzen Vormittag. Derweilen schläft der Brief
im Park und die Soldaten darauf.

Wenn der Zug kommt fährt dein Brief mit den vielen
anderen Briefen im Park mit den Soldaten im Zug bis in
die nächste Stadt.

Dort sind schon viele Briefsäcke von vielen mit Briefen.
Alle zusammen werden in einen neuen Zug geladen
und dann fahren ganz ganz schnell bis nach Deutschland
bis nach Berlin

Then the sack is carried to the train station, and then there's a wait until the train comes. One hour, two hours, a whole morning. Meanwhile the letter sleeps in the sack, and the soldiers sleep on top of it.

When the train comes, your letter and all the other letters in the sack go with the soldiers by train to the next town. There, many heaps of sacks full of letters are already waiting. Together they are loaded onto a new train, and then they drive very very fast all the way to Germany, all the way to Berlin,

and still further to Holland, and finally to Amsterdam. But before getting there, this letter has to pass a scary test, and the nearer that frightening hour approaches, the more anxiously its heart beats. Several stern, strict men read and examine it, and if there is nothing bad in it, they paint bright brush strokes on the front and the back of it, stamp it, paste stickers on it, and cover it with mysterious numbers and signs. For the letter, this is as good as a ticket. With a sigh of relief it resumes its voyage. In Amsterdam, it is tossed into a box with the letters ZUID on it. By this time the letter is exhausted from traveling so long, from being opened and shut again, from being packed and unpacked. But then comes a lady who picks it up and drops it in a big pouch, and the moment she does that, the letter feels wide awake again and makes sure to settle on the very top of the heap, for it knows that now it's being taken to its dear little Barbara Philippine. Early in the morning, the lady carrying the letter steps into the number 24 streetcar, gets out at Albrecht-Dürer-Strat,

und noch immer weiter bis nach Holland und dann endlich nach Amsterdam.

doch was kommt für den Brief noch eine weite Stunde, der es nicht ohne Herzklopfen entgegengeht. Von einer Reise...

ZUID

ganz aber nur zu liegen kommt, so wie es jemals, jetzt geht zur kleinen lieben...

geht bis zum Haus №5 und wirft dort den Brief in
den Kasten. Sie findet die Barbara den Brief. Jetzt
ist der Brief da wo er hingehört so wie es auch dem
Couvert steht und dort bei der lüftigen Barbara will
er bleiben.

Die Geschichte vom Brief ist
so lang geworden, daß gar
kein Platz mehr bleibt
um die Geschichte vom
Regen zu erzählen. Wenn
Regen bei die jeden Tag
regnet und alles Wasser
in eine Regenwolke
oder Strom über Donau
hin wandelt. Darum
werde ich dir bis nächst
Mal erzählen. In diesem
Brief will ich dir nur
noch das Regenbildchen
von der alten Dame, dem kleinen Brief, dem
großen Regenschirm und der dicken Kuh zeichnen.

Nur wenn ich zu dir komme
mußt du Sonne scheinen.
Dann darf es nicht regnen
dann kann es nicht süß
mit die spazieren zu gehen
und nicht wieder unnütz
die zuzuhören

Deine
Platschnasse Berger lad.

goes to house number 5, and drops the letter in the box beneath the bell. That is where Barbara finds the letter, and now the letter is where it belongs, at the place that is written on the front of the envelope, and there, with my gay little Barbara, it will remain.

The story of the letter became so long that I have no space left to tell the story of the rain that falls every day and turns all the streets here into deep muddy trenches or streams or brooks. I'll tell you about that the next time. For now, I will draw you a picture of the old woman, the little book, the big umbrella, and the fat cow. But, when I come to see you, we need bright sunlight and no rain, because I want to go for a walk with you and listen to *your* stories.

Your soaking wet Papaleo

Wednesday, the 27th of September, 1943.

My dear little Babbela!

Yesterday was a holiday for me, for yesterday was the day when your dear letter arrived. Did you speak it out loud for Elizabeth to write down exactly the way you said it? Just like a big businessman telling his secretary what to put in a letter? Did you strut around the livingroom with your hands behind your back, the way he would? It really is a specially beautiful letter, and it made me terribly happy. Yes, my dear little one, unfortunately I can't buy you any toys, for there is nothing to buy here. The little children who live here have no toys, and they have no school either. When they want to play, they go to the woods to play hide and seek or to gather wood for the stove and blackberries and mushrooms. At home, the boys and girls play with little horses, the dogs, the cats, and the rabbits.

Am Mittersee, den 27. September 1943

Mein liebes kleines Gerburtstagskind!

Gestern war ein Feiertag für mich, denn gestern kam Dein lieber Brief hier an. Wie ein ganz großer Schulmann hiner Sekretärin, so hast Du ihn der Elisabeth vorgesagt und Elisabeth hat ganz genau aufgeschrieben was Du gesagt hast? Bist Du auch in der Stube herum-
spaziert mit den Händen auf dem Rücken? Es ist aber auch ein besonders schöner Brief geworden und ich hab mich furchtbar damit gefreut.
Ja, mein liebes Kleines, heimlich kann ich Dir lieber lieber keines kaufen, denn hier gibt es nichts zu kaufen.

(Speech bubble:) Lieber Peppi!

Die kleinen Kinder, die hier wohnen haben gar keine Spielsachen und auch keine Schule.

Wenn sie spielen wollen, gehen sie in den Wald, spielen Versteckten und suchen Holz für den Ofen, Beeren und Pilze.

Zu Hause spielen die Jungen und die Mädchen mit den kleinen Pferdchen, den Hunden, den Katzen und Kaninchen.

Einen Laden gibt es hier doch. In dem Laden sind ein paar Räder, Streichhölzer, einige Nähnadeln und etwas zum Ansehen aus Glasperlen. Ein kleines

Mädchen verkauft die Sachen und dort habe ich ein Andenken für Dich gekauft. Ich habe es in einem Päckchen vor einigen Tagen an Dich abgeschickt.

Dann fragst Du, ob ich im nächsten Brief mich selbst mal zeichnen will. Liebe Babsy, das ist mir sehr schwer — und seht habe ich auch schon ganz schnell das Zeugzeichnen, wie ich am liebsten wieder wegmachen möchte. Aber das geht nicht so mich so dem sehen bleiben die die wie er nicht aussieht. Dafür zeichne

ich dir noch einen der ihn der schläft und einen der

wacht, schläft und an die liebe Barbara in Amsterdam denkt. Der Brief ist schon wieder vollgeschrieben. Ich habe gerade noch Platz um

viele viele Grüße und Küsse für dich herauszuschreiben. Der Mama gibt Du bitte von Allem etwas ab. Heute unterschreibe ich diesen Brief so wie du den Deinen, liebe kleine Barbara Philippine Weber, nicht mit Papa lac sondern ganz feierlich mit meinem ganzen Namen.

Liebe Alicia, viele tausend Küsse von Deinem

Leopold August Longin Weber

But there is one store here. In this store are a few matchboxes, some sewing needles, and about ten little necklaces made of glass beads. A little girl sells these things, and that's where I bought a necklace for you. I sent it off to you in a package a few days ago.

You also asked me to draw a picture of me. Dear Babusch, that is very difficult—and now I just drew something very quickly which I wish I could wipe away again. But I can't, so he'll have to stay there, this is Leo the way he doesn't look. To make up for that, I'll draw you another, sleeping, Leo, and a third one standing guard and thinking of his dear Barbara in Amsterdam. This letter is filling up to the edge again. I have just enough space to write many, many greetings and kisses for you. Please share some of these with your Mama. Today I shall solemnly sign this letter, not with Papaleo, but the way you signed yours, dear little Barbara Philippine Meter, with my whole name.

Dear little one, many thousand kisses from your
Leopold August Longin Meter

Letter from Barbara to her father, dictated to her mother. The handwritten original no longer exists.
Amsterdam, October 19, 1943.

Dear Papaleo,

I love you up to the sky and much more, up to the clouds and up until after the war. I'm holding a pipe made out of a chestnut. In the mornings I eat cold cereal, in the evenings I eat a hot meal, and for lunch I eat bread. The letter you made is very beautiful and I think it's very nice that you sent me a necklace in a package. I think it's nice and funny too, that you drew yourself the way you don't look. I took a punt across the Amstel river with Mickie, and of course we found chestnuts on the ground beneath the chestnut tree. Signia-Alma and her Mama Li were here today, and I played with Signia on the balcony in the sun. And then we ate together at the table in the sun, I drank milk with coffee and Signia did too. *Verder niks* (nothing else). Many kisses, and you should come soon, to the balcony in the sun.

Many greetings and kisses from Barbara

Ausschnitt
aus dem Brief vom
27. September 1943

On the 24th of November, a month before Christmas.

My dear little Barbara,

Today I want to tell you about Edward, the little black pig, and the Christ child. Edward is completely black, funny, playful, and awfully curious. All day long he plays with our white puppy. The puppy bites Edward's snout and his skinny black legs, but the part of Edward he likes to bite most of all is his frisky, curly tail. Edward doesn't mind, and when he's had enough, he'll give the fresh little puppy a push with his nose and send it sprawling and rolling all over the wet sand. Edward's most striking quality is his curiosity. He sniffs and roots up whatever he finds, wherever he is: in the garbage, among the horses, the geese, and the chickens. With a grunt he'll go trotting after any soldier who crosses the yard. In short, he pokes his nose into everyone's business.

Edward is very sociable, he hates being alone. But once, on a dark, cold winter night, Edward walked all alone through the deep snow. He was lost, he was unhappy, he longed for people and warmth. He was crying so much and sobbing so loudly, he didn't see the bright warm light by the edge of the forest and didn't hear the beautiful singing. But he smelled something: delicious milk soup. And that gave Edward courage again, and more and more cheerfully he followed his nose. He trotted along for a little while, and then he saw many shepherds. The men, women, and children were sitting around a big, warm fire, singing a beautiful song, surrounded by many hundreds of sheep. The song was about a little child that was born on that night. The child was very small and was sleeping on the straw, its parents were poor, and the winter was cold. The shepherds wanted to look for the child. The women fetched diapers and food,

Meine liebe kleine Großbauer,

Heute will ich dir etwas erzählen von dem kleinen schwarzen Schweinchen.

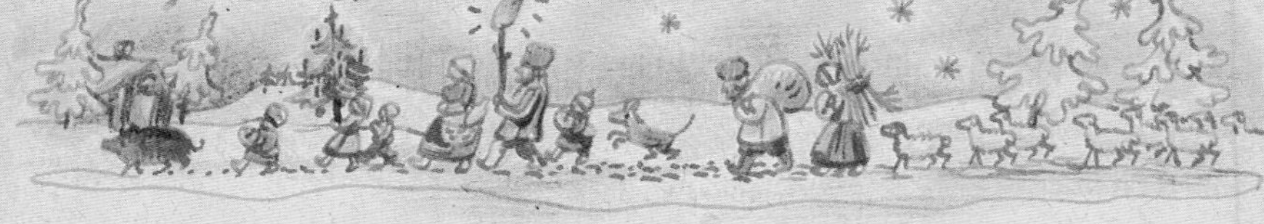

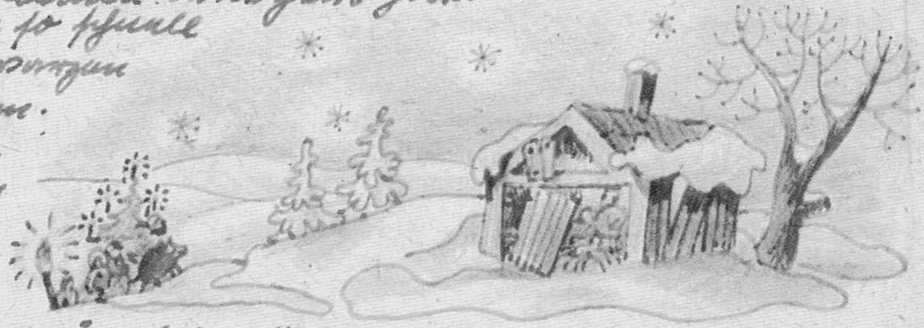

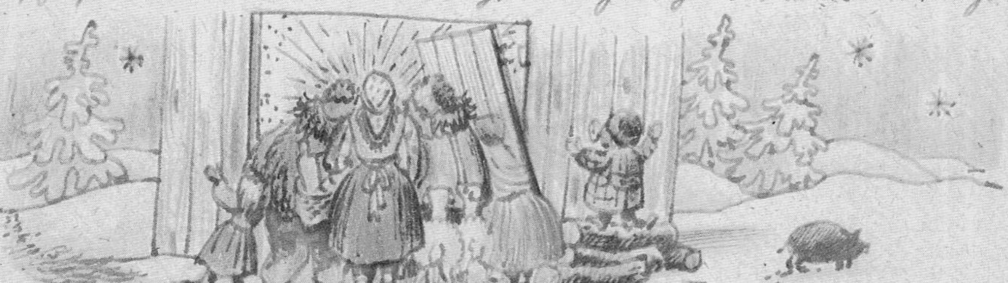

the men lit torches, and the children carried a bright Christmas tree. And so they set out to find the little child. They wanted to bring it all those lovely presents.

And Edward? Edward had forgotten his hunger and also the cold. He was trotting ahead of the others, leading the way. Again he relied on his nose, and he also listened with his ears and peered with his eyes as hard as he could. So it was no wonder at all that he smelled the poor people's thin soup from afar and saw the weak light of the candle glimmering through the cracks of the old manger and heard the soft crying of the little child. Then he ran as fast as his short black legs could carry him. And following behind him, slipping and running and leaping and sliding through the snow, came the shepherds and shepherdesses with their loads and all their children and the many hundreds of sheep. But they all ran much faster than Edward, and most unfortunately, just before reaching the manger, he slipped. He was the last to arrive at the door. He couldn't pass through the thick forest of legs— human legs and sheep legs—and he couldn't see anything. Oh, how deeply unhappy Edward was. He turned away from the manger and left, and he was about to cry again.

But listen, what is that sound? That marvelous faraway sound of music and strange instruments? And what are those rare smells, and those red, blue, green, yellow, and white glimmers and flashes in the dark distance? And that light traveling through the sky—isn't that a star no one has ever seen before, and aren't those lights, sounds, and smells following behind it? What could it be? Where is it all going? But this is something Edward can't find out without looking for himself. I have already told you, dear Babella, that Edward is tremendously curious. Driven by his curiosity, he runs and stumbles again through the snow in the direction of the light.

Soon his little legs can no longer carry him, because he has been running for so long. All heated up and pitch black he sits in the cold white snow, but with his little eyes he's still peering out at the light. He sees it coming closer. Straight up to him. After a while—Edward doesn't believe his eyes—three kings approach him, wearing scarlet gowns around their shoulders and golden crowns on their heads. The first king, a venerable old man with a long white beard, stops his horse and asks—but Edward already knows what these rich people want. They, too, are looking for the little child and want to bring it gold and other precious gifts. Edward is already running to show them the way. But now he's not running so fast. He is tired. And besides, there's so much to look at. Not only is there the king with the long white beard,

Horch, was ist das?, hört er nicht in der Ferne herrliches Klingeln
und Rauschen von fremden Instrumenten, riecht er nicht die
seltensten Gerüche und sieht er nicht in der dunklen Ferne
rotes, blaues, grünes, gelbes und weißes Blitzen, Glitzern
und Schimmern? Kommt nicht das Zimmern aus der geheimnis-
vollen und ziehen die ersten, die zweiten und die dritten nicht
hinter ihm her? Was kann das sein? Wo geht es hin?
Das kann Schwanold aber nicht genau wissen kann er selbst
hingeht. Ich habe dir schon erzählt, lieber Habbalar, daß
Schwanold ungeheuer neugierig ist. Von einem Räuschende
getrieben läuft und folgt er schon weiter durch den
tiefen Schnee dem Licht entgegen. Bald tragen ihn seine
Beine gar nicht mehr, so weit ist er schon gelaufen in dieser
Nacht. Feucht und schwarz sieht er im kalten weißen Schnee,

doch mit seinen kleinen Äuglein schaut er noch immer ins nach
dem Licht. Er fängt es nachzukommen. Genau ist ihn zu.
Doch einer Weile — Schwanold traut seinen Augen nicht —
kommen drei Könige mit goldenen Kronen und
Königsmänteln. Der erste König, ein würdiger
alter Mann mit einem
langen weißen Bart hält sein Pferd
an und fragt — aber Schwanold
weiß schon was die reichen
Leute wollen. Auch sie suchen
das kleine Kind und
wollen ihm gold und
Güte und seltene Dinge
bringen und unser armer
Schwanold läuft schon weiter um
den Weg zu zeigen. Doch jetzt
geht es nicht mehr so schnelle, so
ist müde. Auch hat er so weit
zu gehen. Da ist nicht mehr der
König mit dem langen weißen Bart.

sondern auch noch ein brauner König. er reitet auf einem
Camel und schaut immer zum Himmel nach dem Stern und
zuletzt sitzt auf einem großen Elefant ein König der ist ganz
so schwarz wie Eduard. Immer wieder muß Eduard dahin
gucken. Der schwarze König ließ ihn zu und Eduard freut sich.
Sie sind sie alle schon ob zu innersten zum Stall gekommen.
die vorigen Heiligen ab, gehen in den Stall. Die treten manchen
Platz und auch Eduard kann endlich in den Stall hineingehen.
Hier ist es schön worden. Der Weihnachtsbaum brennt. Die Hirten
und die Könige machen Musik und singen schön alte Lieder.
Jeder hat was ab bekommen zu essen. Eduard bekommt auch
etwas. er weiß gewiß nicht ob er zuerst hinschauen soll. Da bleibt
er dann zum erstenmal still und bescheiden auf seinem
Platz sitzen. Da kommt der schwarze König und nimmt
Eduard auf den. Nun der kann er jetzt alles sehen.
Das kleine Kindchen in der Krippe, auf Heu und auf Stroh,
der Vater Joseph und die Mutter Maria, die Ochsen und
den Esel, die Schäfchen die Hirten und Könige.

Eduard ist glücklich. Diese Nacht die
Nach vom 24. zum 25. Dezember wird er nie vergessen.
Und wenn die Nacht jetzt wieder kommt wird ein jeder
lieber kleiner Lausbube denken sein Tagebuch.

there's also a brown king. He is riding on a camel, and he keeps gazing at the star in the sky. Behind him, on an elephant, sits a third king who is just as black as Edward, and he's the one Edward just can't take his eyes off. The black king greets Edward with a laugh, and Edward is glad.

And suddenly, unexpectedly, they arrive at the manger. The kings climb off their mounts and go into the manger. The shepherds make room for them. It is nice and warm inside. The candles on the Christmas tree are lit. The shepherds and the kings make music and sing ancient songs. Everyone gets something tasty to eat. Edward too. He doesn't know where to look first. And so, for the first time, he just remains modestly seated right where he is. Then the black king comes and lifts Edward up in his arms. Now he has a wonderful view of everything in the manger. He sees the little child bedded on hay and straw in the crib, he sees the child's father, Joseph, and the child's mother, Mary, and the oxen, and the donkey, and the little sheep, the shepherds, and the kings. Edward is happy. He will never forget this night, the night of the 24th to the 25th of December. And when that night comes back again soon, he will think of his dear little Babbela.

Your Papaleo

This Pan and his whole family
wish you, dear little Babbela,
a joyful, merry Christmas, and so does
your Papaleo.

Afterword

My father, Leo Meter, was born in Cologne in 1911. He came from a family of socialists and artists. His father was an opera singer. Already at the age of twelve, he received his first lessons in painting and drawing at the set design workshop of the Cologne opera house. Later he studied with Heinrich Camperdonk, who taught at the art academy of Dusseldorf from 1922 until 1933, when he was dismissed from his post and went into exile. In 1932 Leo Meter became a set designer and directorial assistant at the *Junge Volksbuhne* in Berlin, a theater of leftist political orientation that was also one of the first to use children as actors. He designed and helped distribute antifascist posters for the Socialist Youth Movement. In 1933 everyone who worked for the *Junge Volksbuhne* was arrested by the Nazis. My father was sent to the concentration camp at Brauweiler near Cologne. After his release he was officially forbidden to practice his profession. He received no unemployment benefits and had to report to the police every day.

In 1934 he was able to flee to Amsterdam, where he met my mother. My mother, Elisabeth Plaut, was Jewish and had fled to Amsterdam to escape persecution in Germany. Since foreigners in Amsterdam were bound by the laws of their country of origin, and since in Germany a ''mixed'' marriage between Jews and ''Arians'' was forbidden, they were married in Brussels in 1936. I was born in Amsterdam in 1939. There my mother worked as a teacher. Leo illustrated books and worked at the children's theater, *De vrolikje Brigade* (the Cheerful Brigade). When the Nazis occupied Holland in 1940, my mother and my father had to divorce in accordance with the Nazi race laws. From then on, my father no longer lived with us—but he visited us every day. He lived in a room on the Prinsengracht in the Old City of Amsterdam—next to the house

where Anne Frank was hidden. He worked in the resistance movement. Not until after the war did we learn that he helped Jews to cross the border with his passport. In the summer of 1942, my mother and I had to leave our apartment at Albrecht Durer street and move into the "open ghetto" in North Amsterdam. In December of the same year, my father was arrested. Three months later, the Gestapo delivered him to the Wehrmacht, the German army. His company was sent to the Ukraine, and that is where he wrote the "letters to Barbara."

Because I was a "half-Arian" child, my mother and I were allowed to return to our apartment on Albrecht Dürer street. That was where I received the letters from my father. Unfortunately I can't remember that. My mother told me later that I was always asking about "Papaleo." He was my great love, and that love was mutual! For I can still remember my father. He was always cheerful, as far as I know, and he always spoiled me. When my father came into the small dark apartment in *Asterdorp* (that was the name of the open ghetto), it was as if the sun were rising. He would pick me up and laugh with me. In *Distant Closeness*, the film I made in 1983, I tried to translate these memories into images.

At the end of 1943, my mother and I were forced to separate and go underground. I was sent to live with a family in Overijsel in eastern Holland. There, too, according to letters written by my foster family, I talked a lot about my "Papaleo." I also named my doll Leo. My mother kept moving from one address to another. She survived the war and died at eighty years old in February 1987.

My father's last letter was written in the winter of 1943. On July 26, 1944, he fell in action in Poland—or else he was shot. We don't know. He was note quite thirty-five years old. My father was a "bad soldier." A soldier from my father's company visited my mother after the war and

told her that when my father was ordered to shoot at the enemy, he shot into the air. It could be that he was killed for that reason.

I would have given anything to get my father back. I am proud of my father. I am proud of who he was and the kind of person he was and the way his letters and drawings express his nature. And that he shot into the air.

A note about the letters
The reproductions of the letters are slightly reduced in size. The penciled numbers on the letters were added by the censors; the blue stripes signify that the letter has passed inspection.

First published in the United States in 1995 by
The Overlook Press
Lewis Hollow Road
Woodstock, New York 12498

Library of Congress Cataloging-in-Publication Data

Meter, Leo
[Briefe an Barbara. English]
Letters to Barbara/Leo Meter; translated by Joel Agee.
p. cm.
1. Meter, Leo—Correspondence 2. Meter, Leo—Relations with Jews.
3. World War, 1939-45—personal narratives, German. 4. Jews—
Netherlands—Persecutions. 5. Jewish children—Netherlands—
Correspondence. 6. Soldiers—Germany—Biography.
I. Meter, Barbara. II. Agee, Joel. III. Title.
D811.M4818 1995
940.54'8243—dc20
[B]   94-46275   CIP

ISBN:0-87951-589-9
First American Edition
135798642